Breathe
Dreams
Exhale
Wonders

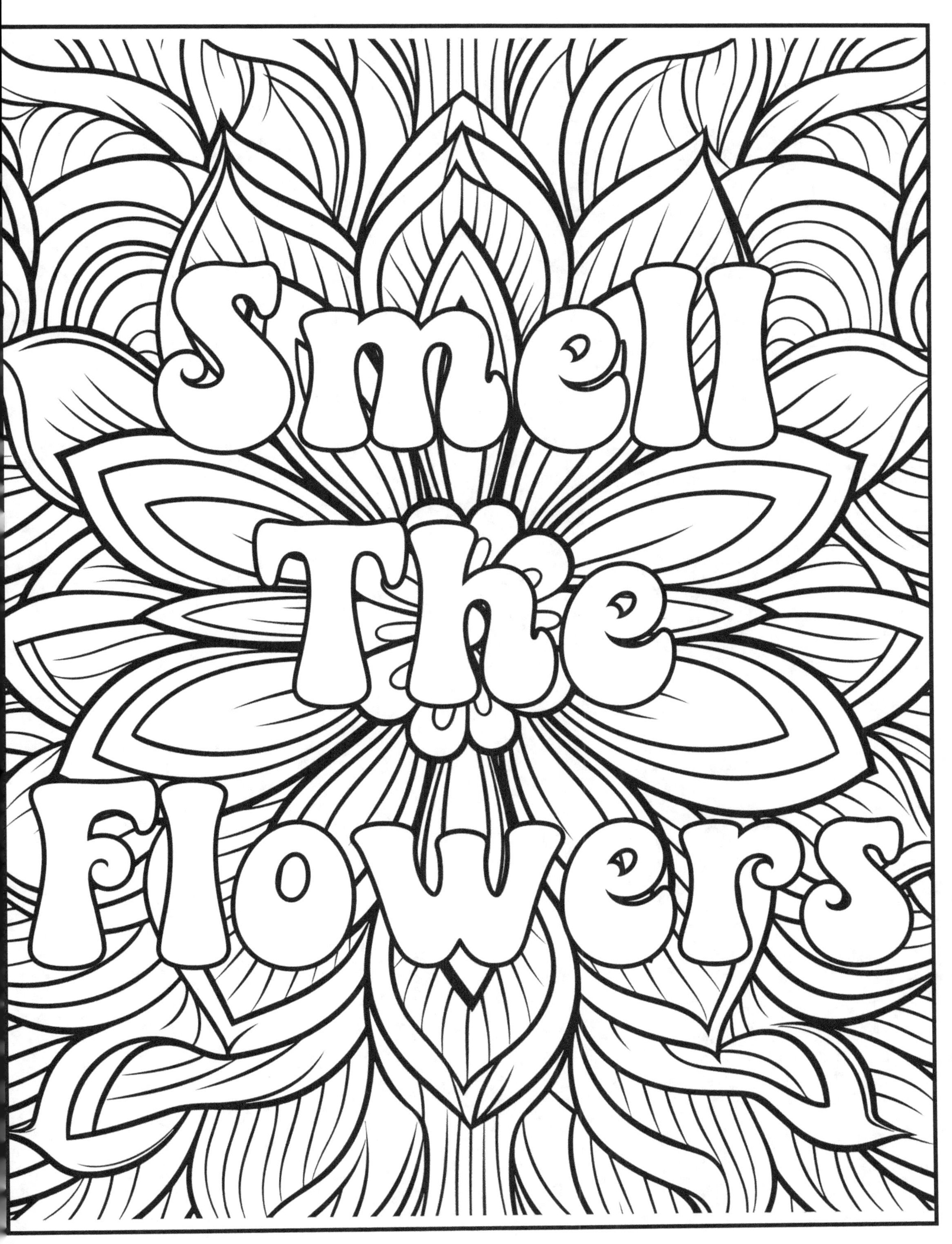

Smell
The
Flowers

Stars
Above
Roots
Below

Flower
Power
Forever

Life
Is
A
Wild
Ride

WHISPERED
WISHES
ON
WINDS

Ebb
And
Flow
With
Fate

Let
Your
Soul
Sing

BEYOND
BOUNDS
BECKONS
BEAUTY

Every
Moment
A
Miracle

Nature
Is
The
Best
Medicine

HIPPIE
HEARTS
UNITE

Dreams
Painted
In
Hope

Harmonize
With
Life's
Symphony

Harbor
Hopes
Harness
Heavens

Eternal
Echoes
Of
Ethereal
Energy

Trust The Cosmic Journey

Life
Is
For
Loving

Peace
Signs
And
Tie
Dye

KEEP
PEACE
IN
YOUR
SOUL

CELESTIAL
SIGHTS
HEART'S
HORIZONS

Drenched
In
Cosmic
Colors

Dance In The Rain

Between
Stars
Find
Stories

Living
free
Loving
All

MOUNTAINS
ECHO
SILENT
DREAMS

SKY
ABOVE
EARTH
BELOW

Wander
With
Heart's
Whispers

Eclipsing
Fear
With
Love

Keep
The
Love
Flowing

Vibes
Of
Peace
Expand

Celestial
Dreams
Earthly
Bonds

Keep
The
Soul
Wild

Dive
Into
Dreams
Swim
In
Stars

Flow
With
Life's
Currents

Flower
Child
Spirit

Living
Wild
Loving
Kind

Dance
Amidst
The
Stars

One
Love
One
Life

BREATHING
DREAMS
LIKE
AIR

HARMONIZE
WITH
THE
HEAVENS

Trust The Process

Vibes
Of
Unity
Resonate

Moon's
Muse
Sun's
Serenade